AF479950

This is a ball
of very hot gas,

a big giant Sol

with a whole lot of mass.

A heavy, hot star,
shining so **bright**,

you can see from afar,
at least when it's **night**.

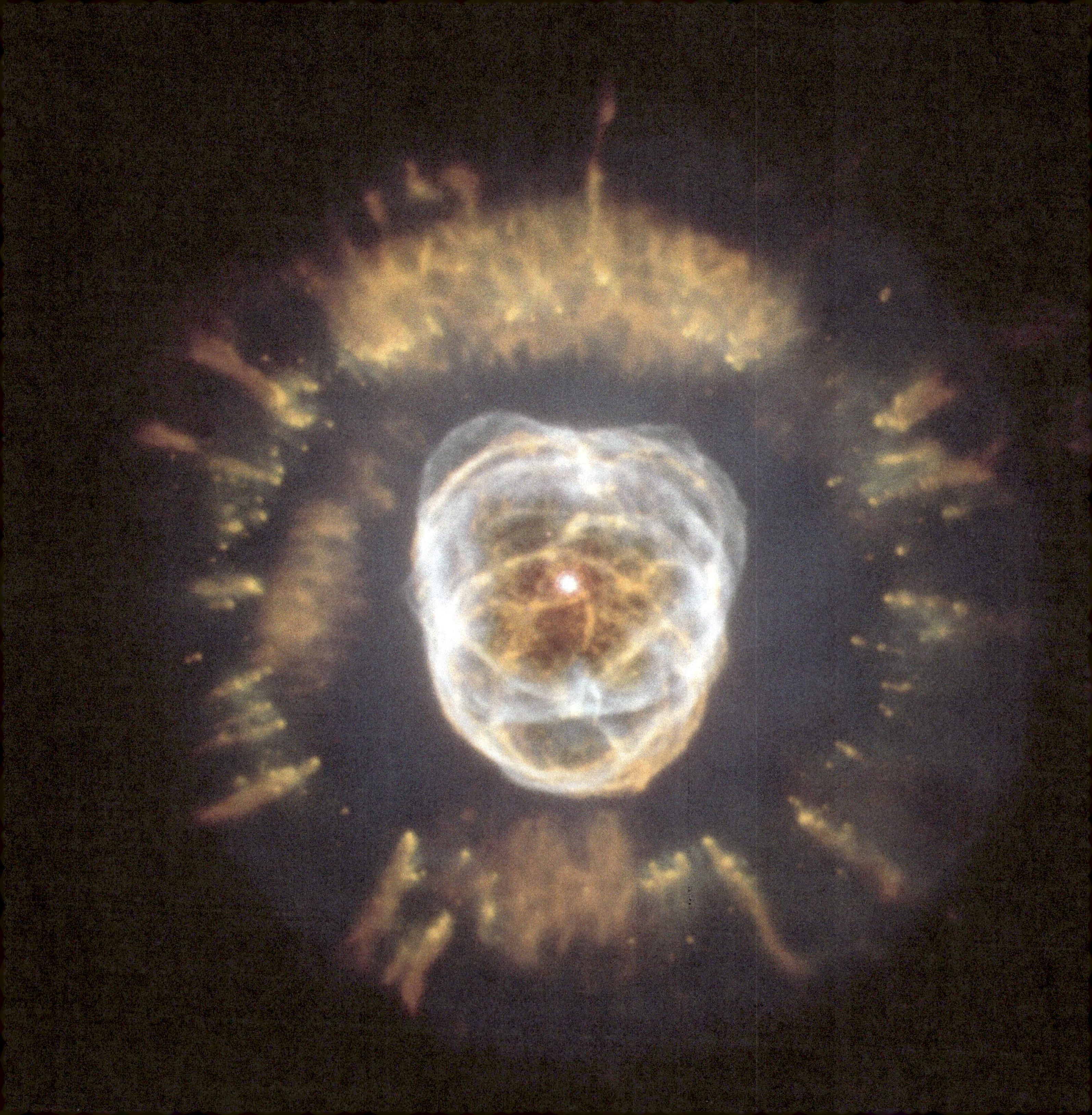

The light from this star
also *pushes* the gas.

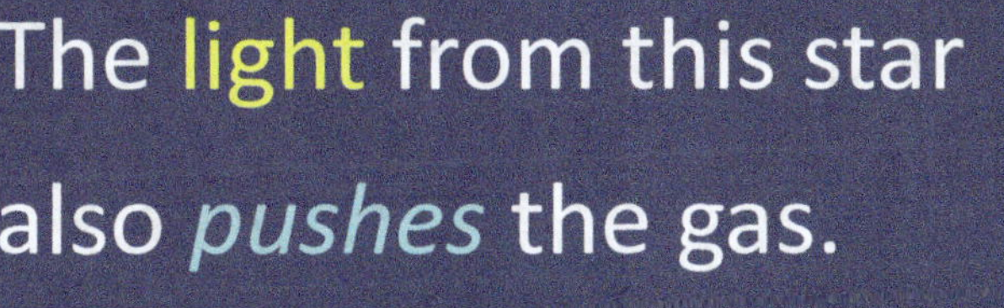

Like a superhot car,
it makes it go *fast*.

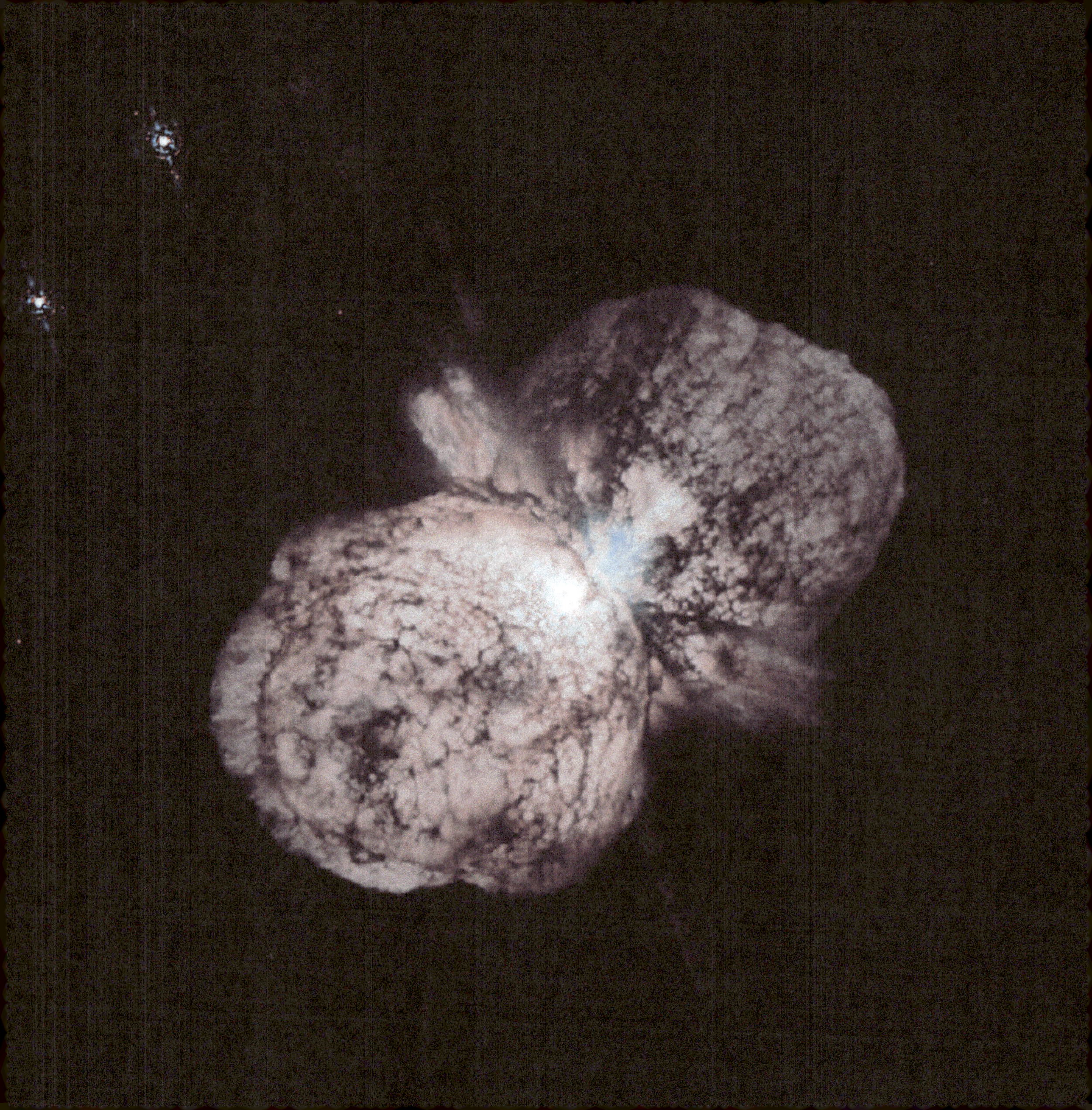

The gas from the top
is lost into space...

and never does stop,
just keeps on its pace.

This wind like a shroud
casts the star in big trouble.

In the neighboring cloud
it just blows a big *bubble*.

As the top layers are shed
the core starts to shrink,

as it loses its head,
ever smaller to *slink*.

It still is a ball,
but not nearly so massive.

It's gotten quite small,
but hardly is passive.

For inside this core
the atoms are pushed.

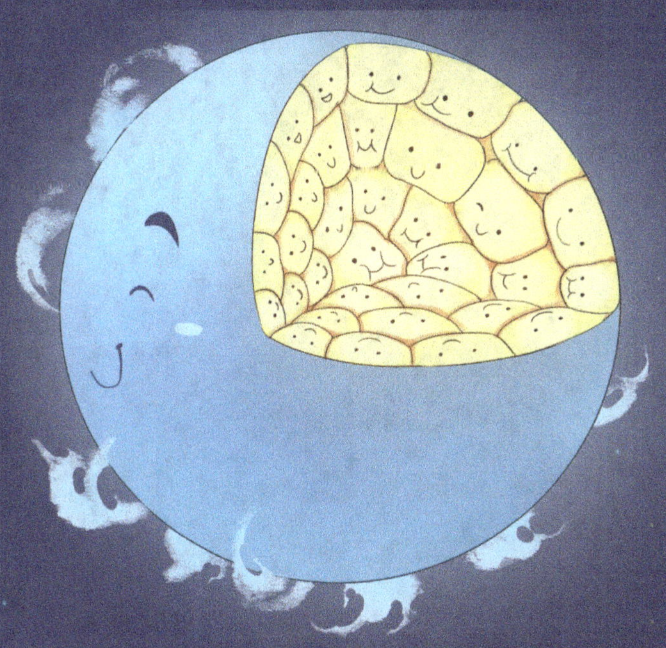

Making one out of more,

they really get *smushed*.

Onward this goes

till the core gets so *heavy*

that *downward* it flows,

like the break of a levee.

As its inside implodes,
the star just explodes,

then *bounces* back over,
a collapse *supernova*!

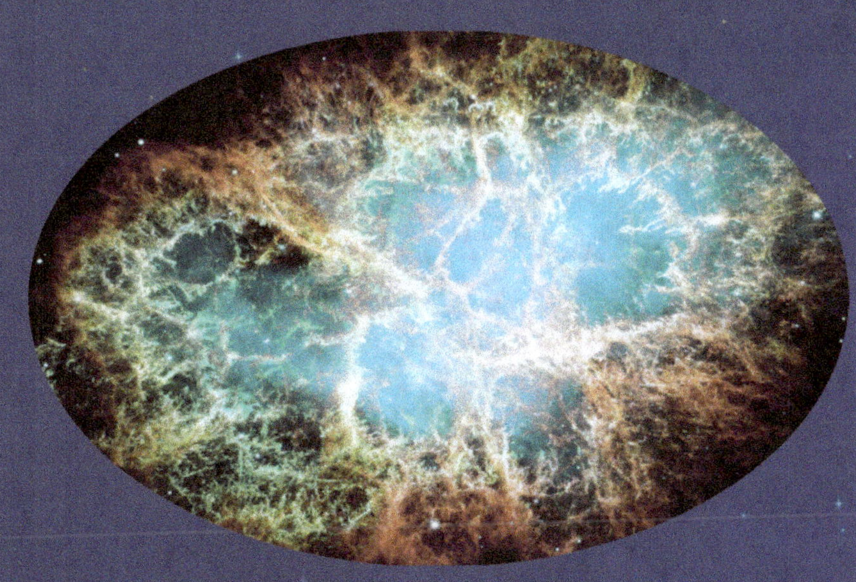

This spits complex atoms back out into space, where with eons of add-ons they made your cute face.

Thus Big Stars helped you
become what you are,

so are reborn anew

in you, little star!

www.ingramcontent.com/pod-product-compliance
Lightning Source LLC
Chambersburg PA
CBHW081057140726
48009CB00014B/203